For

_____

I always thank God for you.

1 CORINTHIANS 1:4

From

_____

Grandmas are a Gift from God
© 2002 by The Zondervan Corporation

ISBN 0-310-80800-6

Compiler: Molly C. Detweiler
Cover Design: Mark Veldheer
Interior Design: Kris Nelson
Illustration: Lyn Boyer Nelles

Printed in China
04 05 06/HK/5 4 3 2 1

Grandmas
are a
Gift from God

inspirio™

The gift group of Zondervan

A grandma's love
is a glimpse
of heaven.

I Love Visiting Grandma
because...

She lets me run in the house.

She collects sand dollars from the sea and makes them white.

She lets me sleep overnight at her house.

She makes Mickey Mouse waffles from scratch, not the kind from the freezer.

She plays games with me.

She takes naps when I do.

She makes meat that's easy to chew.

She listens to me read.

She lets me drink soda pop.

She lets me read in bed way past my bedtime.

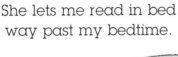

The wisdom of a grandmother
is in her patience. Her gentle
silence induces a confession of
guilt in less than three minutes.

DORIS RIKKERS

One of the most influential
handclasps is that of a
grandchild around the
finger of a grandparent.

AUTHOR UNKNOWN

A grandmother doesn't have to
do anything. Just knowing that
she's somewhere thinking of
you means everything.

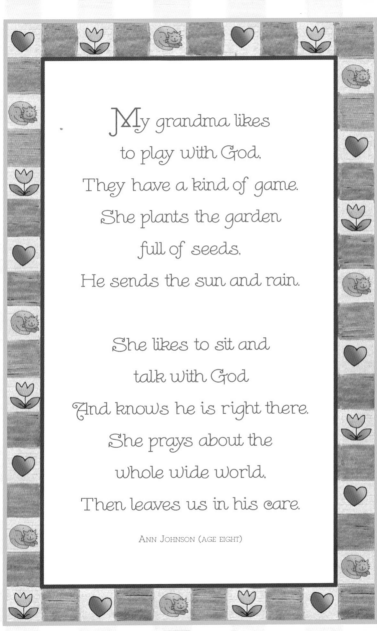

My grandma likes
to play with God.
They have a kind of game.
She plants the garden
full of seeds.
He sends the sun and rain.

She likes to sit and
talk with God
And knows he is right there.
She prays about the
whole wide world.
Then leaves us in his care.

ANN JOHNSON (AGE EIGHT)

What is a Grandmother?

A grandmother is a combination of work-worn hands, after a lifetime of toil, a loving heart, and endless stories of the days when her family was young.

You don't notice what grandmothers wear, you only see the love and tenderness in her face as she cuddles her youngest grandchild.

Grandmothers have spent a whole lifetime cooking meals that statisticians would be unable to record, keeping house, helping neighbors, and drying the tears of the past generation as well as the present.

Grandmothers can always be counted on to produce sweets, cookies and candies that seem to taste nicer from her than from anyone else.

The nicest possible place to hear a story is in Grandmother's lap. Giants and ogres hold no terrors when you are held in the warmth and love of a grandmother with your head pillowed on her shoulder.

Grandmothers just don't believe that their grandchildren have any faults. They can be relied upon to champion the underdog and lost causes. When a chap is in trouble for not washing behind the ears, she will console him by telling him that his dad was almost nine before he overcame that problem.

Grandmothers can soothe an unruly, weeping young boy or girl just by rocking them on her lap and crooning in a soft voice.

Grandmothers give the impression of being all wisdom and love whether in giving help or advice to a neighbor or making a hurt finger better with a kiss.

ELIZABETH FAYE

*I will sing of the Lᴏʀᴅ's great love forever;
with my mouth I will make your
faithfulness known through all generations.*

Psᴀʟᴍ 89:1

*God gives strength to the weary
and increases the power of the weak. ...
Those who hope in the Lᴏʀᴅ
will renew their strength.
They will soar on wings like eagles;
they will run and not grow weary,
they will walk and not be faint.*

Isᴀɪᴀʜ 40:29, 31

The greatest gift a grandmother can give her grandchildren is her faith.

After a day of watching the grandchildren, the Lord renews our strength in a very practical way—he lets us send them home.

My grandmother makes me think that God is her best friend.
I hope I can know him that way too.

A garden of love
grows in my
grandmother's heart.

When I stopped the bus to
pick up Chris for preschool,
I noticed an older woman
hugging him as he left the house.

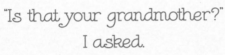

"Is that your grandmother?"
I asked.
"Yes," Chris said. "She's come
to visit us for Christmas."

"How nice," I said.
"Where does she live?"

"At the airport," Chris replied.
"Whenever we want her,
we just go out there and get her."

There's no place like home— except Grandma's!

Grandma's home is her grandchildren's second home, a sort of security blanket they can escape to when the world is unfriendly.

JANET LANESE

The Lord blesses the home of the righteous.

PROVERBS 3:33

Distance cannot diminish a grandmother's love.

Grandmothers are people who keep pictures of their grandchildren up on the walls, even if they don't match the decor.

"I will make you the everlasting pride and the joy of all generations," says the Lord.

Isaiah 60:15

Not only is Nana my best friend, she's
the smartest person in my family.
My mother told me that it only took
Nana one semester of college to hook
grandpa and get her M.R.S. degree.

NICHOLAS (AGE TEN)

My grandma tells me she keeps
the family skeletons in the closet,
but I've looked and looked
and still can't find them.

SARAH (AGE FIVE)

The nicest compliment one
grandmother ever received:
"Grandma, I'll be glad when
I'm as old as you are, so I'll have
as much fun as you do."

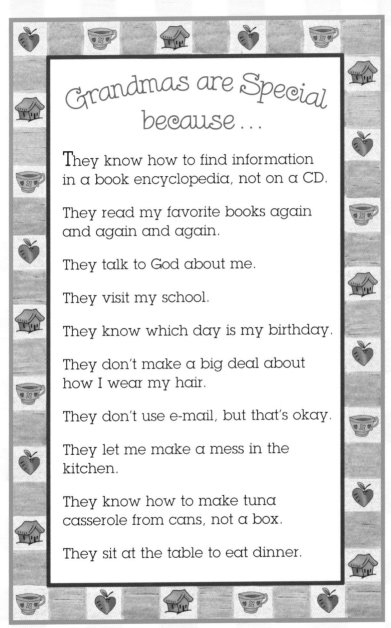

Grandmas are Special because...

They know how to find information in a book encyclopedia, not on a CD.

They read my favorite books again and again and again.

They talk to God about me.

They visit my school.

They know which day is my birthday.

They don't make a big deal about how I wear my hair.

They don't use e-mail, but that's okay.

They let me make a mess in the kitchen.

They know how to make tuna casserole from cans, not a box.

They sit at the table to eat dinner.

I didn't know if my granddaughter
had learned her colors yet, so I
decided to test her. I would point out
something and ask what color it was.
She would tell me and she was
always correct. But it was fun for me,
so I continued. At last, she headed
for the door, saying sagely,
"Grandma, I think you should try
to figure out some of these yourself!"

My grandmother knows about
everything I do—the good stuff
and the bad. But she only
remembers the good stuff.

Grandma Makes Me Feel Good because...

She thinks I'm smarter than I really am.

She laughs at my knock-knock jokes
—even the old ones.

She makes me feel like a grown-up.

She tells me funny stories of when she was little.

She sits down with me to talk.

She thinks I'm clever.

She shows off only the best pictures of me.

She tells me she misses me.

She buys me things that Mom says
are too expensive.

She has an endless supply of kisses.

Grandmas are meant
for kisses and hugs.
For watching rainbows
and catching bugs.
For baking all your favorite things.
For books to read
and songs to sing.

ANONYMOUS

Children's children are a crown to the aged.

PROVERBS 17:6

A Grandma to Treasure

Grandmas are people who won't let you leave their house without taking "a little something" home with you—candy, apples, fresh bread, some yummy leftovers, that antique vase you've always loved, a book they thought you might like ... just about any great thing you can think of!

Grandma, for all the lovely and wonderful gifts you've given me, thank you! But most of all, thanks for loving me with your whole heart. That is what I will always treasure!

Grandmas
are moms with
lots of frosting.

AUTHOR UNKNOWN

What is a Grandma?

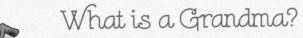

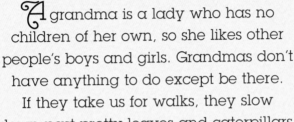

A grandma is a lady who has no children of her own, so she likes other people's boys and girls. Grandmas don't have anything to do except be there. If they take us for walks, they slow down past pretty leaves and caterpillars. They never say "Hurry up." Usually they are fat but not too fat to tie shoes. They wear glasses, and sometimes they can take their teeth out.

They can answer questions like why dogs hate cats and why God isn't married. They don't talk like visitors do which is hard to understand. When they read to us, they don't skip words or mind if it is the same story again. Everybody should try to have a grandma, especially if you don't have televisions, because grandmas are the only grownups who always have time.

AN EIGHT-YEAR-OLD GRANDCHILD

Someone Needs You

If you're feeling low and worthless,
There seems nothing you can do,
Just take courage and remember
There is someone needing you.

You were created for a purpose,
For a part in God's great Plan;
Bear ye one another's burdens,
So fulfill Christ's law to man.

There are many sad and lonely,
And discouraged, not a few,
Who a little cheer are needing,
And there's someone needing you.

Someone needs your faith and courage,
Someone needs your love and prayer,
Someone needs your inspiration,
Thus to help their cross to bear.

Do not think your work is ended,
There is much that you can do,
And as long as you're on earth,
There is someone needing you.

SUSIE B. MARR

Always
remember that
I need you,
Grandma!

25

The Lord your God is with you,
he is mighty to save.
He will take great delight in you,
he will quiet you with his love,
he will rejoice over you with singing.

ZEPHANIAH 3:17

So many times you have helped quiet
my troubled heart with your love.
Thank you for being one of the ways
through which God takes care of me
and shows me his infinite love.

The righteous will flourish like a palm tree,
they will grow like a cedar of Lebanon;
planted in the house of the Lord,
they will flourish in the courts of our God.
They will still bear fruit in old age,
they will stay fresh and green,
proclaiming,
"The Lord is upright; he is my Rock."

PSALM 92:12–15

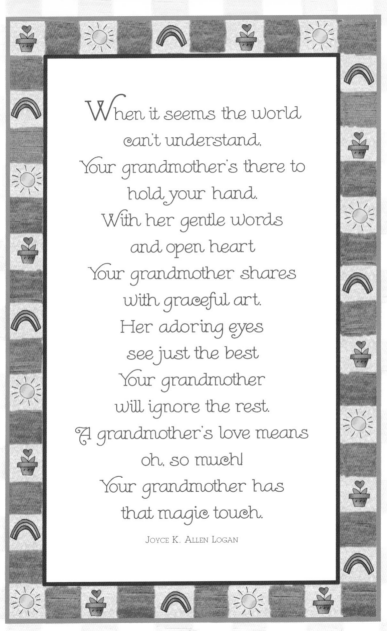

When it seems the world
can't understand,
Your grandmother's there to
hold your hand.
With her gentle words
and open heart
Your grandmother shares
with graceful art.
Her adoring eyes
see just the best
Your grandmother
will ignore the rest.
A grandmother's love means
oh, so much!
Your grandmother has
that magic touch.

JOYCE K. ALLEN LOGAN

You read me Bible stories,
And told me of the good old days;
You showed me that you loved me
In a thousand little ways.

And so I want to thank you
For, Grandma, I hope you see;
You make me feel so special;
You're God's great gift to me!

MOLLY DETWEILER

I will open my mouth in parables,
I will utter hidden things, things from of old—
what we have heard and known,
what our fathers have told us.
We will not hide them from their children;
we will tell the next generation
the praiseworthy deeds of the LORD,
his power, and the wonders he has done.

PSALM 78:2–4

Thank you, Grandma,
for not hiding
God's love from me,
but for showing it to me
in all you do!

A grandmother was surprised by
her seven-year-old grandson one morning
while she visited his home. He had made
her coffee. She drank what was the worst
cup of coffee in her life. When she got to the
bottom, there were three of those
little green army men in the cup.
She said, "Honey, what are these army
men doing in my coffee?"
Her grandson said,
"Grandma, it says on TV
'The best part of waking up
is soldiers in your cup!'"

30

Grandma's Hugs are Made of Love!

Everything my grandma does
is something special made with love.
She takes time to add the extra touch
that says, "I love you very much."

She fixes hurts with a kiss and smile
and tells good stories grandma-style.
It's warm and cozy on her lap
for secret-telling or a nap.

And when I say my prayer at night,
I ask God to bless and hold her tight.
Cause when it comes to giving hugs
my grandma's arms are filled with love!

AUTHOR UNKNOWN

If nothing is going well,
call your grandmother.

ITALIAN PROVERB

Thanks, Grandma…
for providing me with a place
to come or just a listening ear,
when things were going rough.
You were a haven of rest for me
in a sometimes bewildering world.

*God will command his angels
concerning you to guard you
in all your ways; they will lift you up
in their hands, so that you will not
strike your foot against a stone.*

PSALM 91:11–12

Thanks for being my
guardian angel—
one that I can see, hear, and hug!

What are Grandmas For?

Grandmas are for stories
about things of long ago.
Grandmas are for caring
about all the things you know ...
Grandmas are for rocking you
and singing you to sleep,
Grandmas are for giving you
nice memories to keep ...
Grandmas are for knowing
all the things you're dreaming of ...
But, most importantly of all,
grandmas are for love.

AUTHOR UNKNOWN

Grandmothers will
laugh at all your jokes.
and they even have some of their own.
But they will not tell you dumb jokes like
lots of grown people tell.

You can never have enough grandmothers.

MARK RIKKERS

Everything that Grandma cooks tastes
better than what my mom cooks.
That seems strange since she's the one
who taught Mom how to cook.
Maybe it's just a secret Grandma-thing.

KATIE, 6

My grandma smells like
roses and cookies.
I love that smell.

JAMES, 4

One time, while I was staying with my
grandma, I had a stomach ache.
I asked her to pray for it and she did
right away. I felt better really fast!
I think Grandma and God are old friends
and she pulled some strings for me.

ETHAN, 7

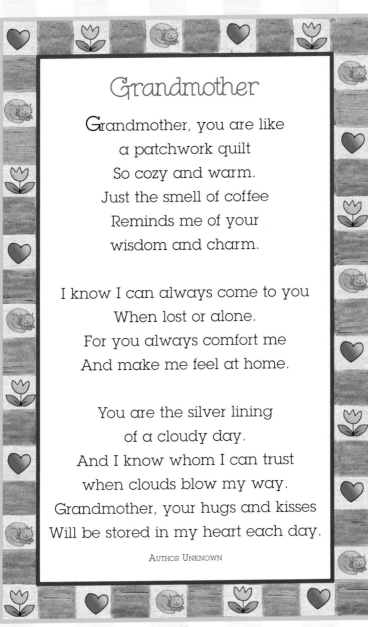

Grandmother

Grandmother, you are like
a patchwork quilt
So cozy and warm.
Just the smell of coffee
Reminds me of your
wisdom and charm.

I know I can always come to you
When lost or alone.
For you always comfort me
And make me feel at home.

You are the silver lining
of a cloudy day.
And I know whom I can trust
when clouds blow my way.
Grandmother, your hugs and kisses
Will be stored in my heart each day.

AUTHOR UNKNOWN

When I'm around you, Grandma, I feel like
a superstar. Everything I do is great and you
think everyone should know that. I may act
embarrassed, but inside I'm loving it!

Grandma, did you know that I'm the richest
person in the world? It's true. I have the
wisdom you have given me, which is worth
far more than rubies. I have the skills you
taught me that are better than silver.
And, I have your unconditional love,
which is finer than the purest gold.
Thank you for this inheritance
that will last forever!

It's such a grand thing to be a
mother of a mother—
that's why the world
calls her grandmother.

AUTHOR UNKNOWN

"Grand"ma is the perfect name for you
because grand means:

Having more importance than others
*(Playing with friends is nice,
but playing with Grandma is the best!)*

Having higher rank than others bearing the
same general designation
*(You know what they say—
"If Mom says no, ask Grandma!")*

Marked by a regal form and dignity
(You're the queen of my heart!)

Very good
(You sure are!)

Grandmother—
a wonderful mother with lots of practice.

When God created grandmas
The world was truly blessed
With all the special joys
That make families happiest.
For grandmas know how to do
The things that warm the heart;
They touch our lives with loving care
Right from the very start.
They show that they believe in us
And all we're dreaming of:
When God created grandmas
He blessed our lives with love.

AUTHOR UNKNOWN

Grandma

I really feel quite special
That God has chosen you.
To be a person in my life
Who knows me through and through.

The time that we spend talking,
I've always felt you heard ...
You've been so good at listening
To each and every word.

And even things I didn't share,
You somehow heard them too.
I think this is a special gift
That God has given you.

So I just want to thank you
For being there for me,
And showing me acceptance
And love so totally.

AUTHOR UNKNOWN

No cowboy was ever
faster on the draw than
a grandma pulling a baby
picture out of her purse.

Author Unknown

I Love You, Grandma

I love you, Grandma,
for your eyes that
shine with pride when you see me,
for your ears that
always have time to hear me,
for your hands that
never cease to soothe me,
and for your heart that
has always loved me.

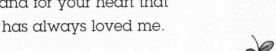

A grandmother is a
babysitter who watches
the kids instead of the television.

AUTHOR UNKNOWN

I praise God because of you,
Grandma. You're so special to
me and I am so grateful to God
that he put you into my life!

Ever since the day I was born.
You have nurtured me with love and kindness.
You have been someone I can believe in,
And someone I can depend upon in
this world I am just starting to understand.
And it's important to me that you know
How grateful that I am,
For all that you give to me,
For all that you teach me,
And for the strength I will always have,
Because of you, Grandma.

AUTHOR UNKNOWN

If becoming a grandmother
was only a matter of choice,
I should advise every one of you
straight away to become one.
There is no fun for old people like it!

HANNAH WHITHALL SMITH

The Lord has done great things
for us and we are filled with joy.

PSALM 126:3

Grandmas are angels
living on earth.

The Lord bless you
and keep you;
the Lord make his face
shine upon you
and be gracious to you;
the Lord turn his face
toward you
and give you peace.

Numbers 6:24–26

Home is where
my grandma is!
I love you, Grandma!